i

c

o

p

e

M

Vint —

le 28 octobre 2014

What a blessing to have you here in NYC for the MacDowell reunion.

Lady Be Good

to MacDowell, to books, to winter, to you!

♡ Lauren Hilger
xoxoxo

LAUREN HILGER

Dear Vint, I need help with my TV? Feathers — more love to you, All my love

CONTENTS

II.

III.

I.

The Announcement

I.

S O M E O N E is trying to kiss my antique mouth. Oh, I distinguish, it's you
—there are no glasses thick enough, darling.

I'm waiting for the others to arrive.
I remember how we walked in that way, numinous

like Bette Davis corseted through her house, martini hello to the gathered.

Her alehouse laugh.

Such order, this black sheath dress, this beaded clutch, a cold bun.
Even and inebriated.

The door opens every night with no hat to hang.

In the black and white Italian movies, the woman is perfect,

but with lipstick and this face, the angle and the mirror of dust, thick
with desuetude,

one sees differently,
which is to say,
not at all.

Inside all the same, Russia's White Sea,

my walk elevated. No one would mourn me like you.

II.

I found myself coming into the hall with a role you've been asking me to accept.

Each time I walk into the room, it's the biggest role yet,
been asked to play the one who feels.

Walking to the table, I get to play the one who is
        newly ready.

At midnight we've nothing to see—we came for the drop.
Get to stand at the top of a chevron of steps.

Only the center of me knows
how alive I am.

How it feels within the mind to play music.
There will be no bonfire, we stay indoors,
play the beat up piano someone managed to drag in by wagon.

Say it again.

It's going to be hard to take apart what was put together so well.

Beneath midnight dots of morning fear being whole.

It is luxury to complain of you
here or not here. I'm here,
far as I know.

III.

The music's slowing down. It's gearing up.
Walk in and out to trumpets—
The mute in the bell of the trombone, the announcement.

Nothing like the stillness once I see you.

Adrenaline yeses through me as though I'd seen a fox.
I leave my valuables anywhere.

A feeling of ivy over me,
a throb of /remember this/
behind the eyes.

Yes, we should do what we can't stomach, give me ribs, let me hold
something even if I'm sleeping.

You can see half this woman's face, the eye.

Claude Thornhill Arrangement

Have the camera blur on his face when he comes back.
Do not be x-acto knife literal.
He makes reference to that stairway right there,
   but there's no point of reference, nothing against
   which to put a person.
Use the weird gas lights from the rooftop bar—this part
   of Brooklyn always reminds him of Greece.
Have him in glasses. He should appear
   village art, grosgrain,
    no matting, sunfaded, a replica.
Put the actress in my heels, demi-pointe;
   have her walk the sidewalks of ice.
She'll ask with eyes down, her birdcage
   fascinator clipped.
She loves the man
who clears his throat
   like the sea in *Beowulf.*
Into the neck of the gramophone,
   she sputters housewife potency.
Have her feel like she is pushing up a bay from under.
Have her bow, and have NY pet her head.
As if it's not enough to be alive,
   she wants to be guided down a staircase.
The ring of bad news is in the outline of the tree branches.
Make up an excuse for them to talk.
Factor in the keyhole of the bedroom door. Factor in they have no key.

Spare a Traveler Some?

If you laugh at some sacred object you change it. Useful onerosity.

Disbelieving and drinking are always present tense. I mean
what is hard and what responds—my horse and her water. I can be
anywhere, I used to think, happy.

Why would anyone travel when you could be in a field
with one person?

When you left, I swallowed a lemon whole.
I didn't know what else to do. I knew
to bless but how among the swanky,
dishonest slobs! I do not say these things about you. "I
am the auto salesman and lóve you." Dear!

I consider not becoming a madwoman. I love a white sky.
Remember when Texas was Mexico? Remember when California
was Mexico? Were we ever wrong in what we believed.

The fire pit has been relocated to a desert museum
barred from the public though it's made of straw and guest towels. Here,

a woman sings me every lyric of KING OF THE ROAD. She
is the mayor of Houston. She knows only one Bucky
and he's dead. What is it that allows you to know symposia

from um—ain't you the poet? Don't leave.
I carry heavy burdens, jrs, carry more than one and have only
ever belonged to a frat across the hall. Perhaps, no, maybe.
The last time I drank all day
I tried to pronounce metallurgist and walked home the wrong way.

Lorn. As in forsaken, desolate, bereft, lovelorn, forlorn. Archaic.
The imperfect, tense with fascination, alive and unmoving.
Allure of my name, spirit heavy. Lure, heavy with spirits.
Gold l'or but with an Au. The lore, all citrus. My name
the verb hidden in the suitcase in my closet.

It Sails Off

When lightning
goes inside you
it doesn't come out,

a decentering
decanter.

Feral
and he's in.

Let me sit in snow
for two hours

with this rein
in my teeth.
Unbutton my glove.

Happen to me.

Hard Hat

Tolstoy is in the cold of Madison Avenue, Christmas lit.
Still a scent of horses, men in ties, a marble intensity.

Pigeons come too close,
scatter wind off the wing
and lovelessness.

I need to go a day without eating
something with Santa's face on the wrapper.

Five pallbearers dump water
from lily bouquets on to the curb's snow.
My suitcase rolls past the hearse and their laughter.

That otherworldly fear, in the way Nietzsche
means otherworldly, simply *not being here.*

This block's under construction,
under hoarfrost and a ledge
that protects with a shadow.

Underground, a woman taps me and says, "Let's go."
I don't know her or her fur turban.
She moves my suitcase to the turnstile
and pays my way in.

She thinks I'm a visitor.
She can see the motherless aura I possess.
Neither is true. Yes they are.

All Dressed

He lifts his hand from the cello like it burns.

Lo, chamber music.

A woman bares her foot in the audience

while he brings the cello to the front of the stage.

He climbs all the way down
and plays it fast as a violin.

There was a time
you would listen to your favorite sonata six times
in your life, should you not play.

The pianist is in a nightblue dress.
I helped fix her barrette when we found each other in the bathroom.

She had asked me, Does the audience want to see the musician's face? I told her, Yes
we should see it, so we pinned a curl by her ear.

When the cellist finishes playing,

he holds his hand above him—the music has to lift off
before he can look at us.

A woman asks him, Can you tell me about your cello?

She's about 250 years old,
he says,

She has a beautiful back, I call her Golda, her face is carved on the scroll,
see?

She has a nice belly. Golda's good to me.
I wish I had more to say about her, to see a face
is not usual.

The Damascus Room

Against the ear a message from one world,
the cold of another, everything lit lurid by
skilled craftsmen. During the day, the escalators keep moving
for no one. There remains that list of the last

things in the life of Prince Nikolay Bolkonsky.
Chapter 6 of *The Last Tycoon*.
Every other page not seen
in the book on display at the museum.

There was a message unmuted,
uninjured, talisman, all ivory hilt,
all of that paper, that manmade
tile, the window.

A seat for everyone—
let's just meet here again.

As Fats Waller as Me

Meyer lemon rind on my lips.

It's very good
no one saw me.

Out on the street, we pass the ripest cherries under a hot light
for sale.

—my arms held out, jacket slipped on,
her fingers fleur de lis, a cigarette placed,

[flower to buttonhole] [hold my drink]
brickwork around us, pin-ups pinned up.

This champagne tastes
like Io's liquid methane,
like sword swallowing.

The feel of stride piano
of manic soul—batwing uncertainty.

I mean, cat, come on, uncare.
Angle your chin, arch your back.

Come on with your prelapsarian, your garden woman,
        the spider plant, salacious, immoderate, rueful, you're not a question.

Problem of Plague

Some of the elements of life
will survive microbial disaster,
will refuse to recognize us,
will come up to the newspapers
and affect a response.

Descartes found himself in the bright blue
strong wind of the northern climate. There,
the erratic queen demanded he give her philosophy
at five in the morning and, calling in a cold,
he died.

On this side of enlightenment,
a bald man combs
his remaining hair for the reading.
He cannot exhale himself
into someone else's mouth. He and I

wish that fresh lemonade
sign were true. Nothing is
promised to everyone. Kant opened a door
he then closed. Still bruised where the watchface sits.
How do I get rid of miasma again? this scary beak of herbs?

stick to my bowler hat? a stick to whack your filth
away from me?
Life too near,
under the blanket, touchy with hate.
We lie in bed, hands on our stomachs like fat professors.

Yet
I am the unscathed lemon.
The sky of me.
The Swiss après-ski
of this face.

Healthy and here.
The nonce. The Entstehung.
How sudden then, as I turn to swoon out, nearly, could have, felt.
What did Dostoevsky smell before
his body betrayed him? Oranges?

Telephone Wire Ring

Reversibly sad.
Fold my laptop, send it down the river.

I think the passage of time means something.

My truck driver buddy does too,
open window in winter, calls me.

We used to be so used to driving
the school bus alone.

Five more minutes, I say every morning,
and wash the salt from my hair.

Birthday

On a stone wall, no one around,
I stare the doe in the face I stole my mom's mink stole

March, my month, cold cake I want this to be the last awful of
white on white winter

my mother sends daffodils that in an open courtyard
are chives unblooming I wait for Jane Kenyon—

thunder over the meadow will we hide how much we love so as to
you allow yourself this appear merely happy

Old Style Russian, March 19, I am like a railroad tycoon with a stack
1805 Lise dies, Prince Nikolay in my hands
is born

how you felt in 6 p.m. sun— my hood
somewhere makes the view a circle

how remarkable the green isn't lurid it's just
if she and her dog were near mossy

would I ever, if not now, be ready for her visit

As Aubrey Beardsley

In Oscar Wilde's *Salome*, the moon is introduced 31 times—
there is nothing in that—
you understand, it's what is not there, what's mute.
When they cut the block they decide what you won't see, there's too much
        hidden already.
And what means more,
the woodcut's space or the dirty fine points?
The moon fell in my drink last night.
It happens when I sit deep in the curve of his life—it won't work out very well
        for either of us,
I'm afraid.
It is wont for me to work until I see it snake
from a remote alley—
like sex coming out of a dark place. Vile eclipse.
What's hiding beneath the overhang
even near the cathedral
in black ink?
Years crawling low in hiding. Sex like we were hiding low.
You understand then,
self-portraits at that stage were of one hand, of a blur in the mirror that
        might've been a back. I thought it would translate today, the message
        blatant. Hide everything that's come before.
This time, I want Salome to be sunlight on the Rhine, want you to dazzle the
        peacock skirt.
The earth is too fast for this—I'm afraid of artists like me, past our small
        prime, ungrateful.
Take this too, I drank from his spoon.
Understand, how can it be blocked?
I learned to sign my name which was the first mistake.

Still-Life of Impractical Items

You want her to hum in your hand,
her skin witching over

as light glints off Salome's carnelian crown, her melted candle,
her vase's thin turquoise lip.

If I understand it correctly,
she is not the ancillary villain
in her life and will not be punished.

Been sitting too close to the clock. It wanted so
badly to strike.

The way the anemone
moves—how you want her heart to move,
to keep touching, to keep moving
like this, outward, fine.

The wind moves your wine.

Officially full, perigee, white and lit. They usher in a cake.

For reasons not fully understood
a low-hanging moon looks this way

when hovering near trees and foreground objects.

The moment is imperceptible
as panic slips under each door.

The amount of torches a test of faith,
and death a heat you can't turn down.

South Street Seaport

I quoted you and my father said no that's Frankl.

The boats down here scare me,
though I walk an hour to see them.

Down Wall Street in chalky August,

the light steals my look and takes it a wavelength above.

I have an unarmed direct gaze.
I have the old world gifts for you,
seven tiny peaches and loose cherries.

Your news reaches me
in a shivering language.

Don't Flinch

First, like a faucet, then
like water in a glass
here to stay full and
refilling—Ask me

to be patient. I'm not.
Fast, run up
the library's roped-off big shot
historical stairs.

Like Tolstoy's Levin
all night before his wedding,
the after winter waving.
I will not stop dancing,

women behind me. As
in Philadelphia, we
got too high, laughed at KANSAS
CITY KITTY, Rudy Vallée,

and sun, and we couldn't leave.
The room an ocean liner.
The dress prewar gold.
The model first edition.

Here to Stay

There's more to this time,   make a mistake.

Let us become younger. I always behave, no need to touch
the electric wire with the back of my hand.
I will grip it with my pulse,

want to fill this space so bring your couch over.

I wear myself on the ship, stand in the courtier's pose,
put on that thunderstorm perfume, it works.

An orange rolled off my table last night—
                             Cézanne thump, the noise made us laugh again.

Like some ship that circles hyphens on an ancient map.

Sit here and inhale that outside cold smoke from somewhere,
preparation for what can't be seen.

Tell me with chiromancy.

An iridescence, (A last state of color you can see
                             before it sinks to black and white)

turns information into heat,
crepitant in the dark. The cause undetermined, details withheld.

The ghost ship arrives.
It siderates you.

You were right here. You could touch my arm.

Red Paisley

I
am the cowboy.

And this man's thin denim's
all I can't see while seated,
a lady, a cat, the forest at night.

The men here

are out to see a face, a geosynchronous object.

I am the body they turn to, contrapposto event.

Dust
pale on my halo.

The shepherd,
shot through with the noble light of neon

and neurophenomenology.

We play all of Art Tatum's
STAY AS SWEET AS YOU ARE
and then once more.

The Platonic What's at Stake

When the weather breaks like this we never talk about it.
It reminds us of a woman.

The form under the small black umbrella
and orange skirt. August.
And you're like this too underneath.
Somewhere you're like this too.
The high waisted skirt makes you walk
like you've something to hide, like you have illicit bites.

Sweating like the grass.
Any idiot with a phone is pretending this is all square,
that if you refresh enough times he'll appear.
Footnotes to him afterward...any philosophy a note to *him*,
the chariot, the charioteer, the two horses.

I have that female hysteria.
I have that no place,
that lost nude, that
expired ID of the loved place,

that I shouldn't be here.

The Platonic what.

The perfect form
of what—

The human form. The Platonic-
sentient form.

The what can't happen happened
and you know it.

As Tolstoy's Natasha on the Hunt

The horse lessens
in my hands.
A portrait
to no one, with hounds.

This fast there's no
sight—as if it's happening
in your body. The palomino
has been shaking all day with this.

Instead of this heart,
I keep packed feathers,
a fat dove's breast, my ribcage.
Musket shouldered, leaves aloft,

I, Natasha, am one who
removes her fur blind periphery
to inhale the woods, to
arrange the fir boughs

over the fireplace for tonight's guests
in the ship-colored room.
We've never lived like this before.
We make decisions off a death-

based tontine. We bet
this sweet life. Remember,
I am not there, not
the wood aflame, the sky unhinged,

lit with coals, the precious call
at the theater, but I grow
to feel the shape of either side,
until the I, too, is let go.

Binary

Algebraically nestled within—
quadratic aquatic magnetic light of the arctic.

Taiga begins where tundra ends—
wherefore conifers confer subarctic.

Computer code allowed it to happen—
trees casting ones/zeros, circling arctic.

Something celadon glazed pale
gray green translucent Antarctic.

Pebbles, a penguin's idea of land.
Take one out, subtrahend Arctic.

We broke into the beach at night.
Women on towels like the arctic moon.

Porcelain Pythia priestess
at the oracle, deliverer of the arctic.

Like there was one way
and the answer, Arctic.

Redux, resurgent, windfall unexpected,
piece of good fortune, as fruit in the arctic.

Exquisite

      when we are the other's,
think of it.

When I carry fewer words.

When we were listening intently
but also watching the cake being spun and iced.

When you played by imagined light
and I leaned into all of it.

At the Met, our papers on the
wooden bench like windows in a brownstone.

Oh my mom,
what's the word for this?

FASCINATING RHYTHM

I was losing so much at first,
I was losing vowels from my own name.

I kept giving up corners.
Fangs of hunger, sugar skull.

Absorbed by the notion of the outlaw,
the imported concept of zero,

that elaborate, that blue, that I could have
left before the thousand pounds of catastrophe.

I'd come to wear the nametag of my ribs.

Pilgrimage

All my life ready, early.
Naked-faced along the highway.
I told one friend, not in English.

Deaths this day along the walk.
Eleven hours the breath of trucks on me.
Felt like a crab waving her claws, like a white sun,

a creature.
Who could I tell of pain
like brandy poured on fire batons.

I carried it and helped it up
and crawled on my knees like everyone else
once we got close enough to the Basilica. It rained.

All electrons,
signaling proteins.
I had nothing with me.

I threw up in a gas station bathroom apple scented.
I bled half the country.
At the steps of the square, we heard a plane overhead.

It flew low enough to shake the Basilica,
to shake us and to drop candy,
for children, ostensibly.

Wanted as Handled

He says the feeling   of picking up
Leda by your beak,   that kind of weight,
imagined, deliriously changed,

is not unlike copying a large amount
of your words and having to remember

to paste them somewhere.
Leda is always placed
with indecorum—

censorial   authentic fat
lawbreaker   masterhood
untested pawn   toughish unity
seemly heroicity   smack,
attacked, attached.

Leda,
the news hard to read,
a promise you make,
a prestige that comes off on you.

Time to be a divine integer.
Time to be the king here

or some other will.

The Top

I thought I'd be on the beach forever,
the wind rippling the umbrella until I caught it with one hand,

in a denim shirt and wet bikini.

Bogie at my wrists,
a firm apricot.

Sometimes it does last.

I'd just been hired and wanted to slap a baton in my hand.

There were open doors everywhere. I unmade the bed

then wore this to the party. I thought like an anarchist,
then wore this to the party. I thought like an anarchist,

with dynamite. The question was written in a hand so fine,
short and for no eyes, or for someone who could answer it—

Last night I touched my own hand to make it close.

I am told I'll make it.
I am the only shirt you need.

As Kitty Scherbatskaya

Here is where it happened, once.

It cut glass at a low and private angle
and sucked sound and I was left there.

In this scene I am razed and ungallant.
My hair contains a line of light.

It is how I am living,
and a shock to see my face through it.

Through my image once and then again,
I pass my hand—what was there goes away.

Each minute gains,
I tan the side of this space.

I'm fine all day

Buried

until I am again in that ream of light,
ruddy in the ballroom
with a burnished expectancy.

Not released from predation pressure,
I simplified my display behavior —

I gave him a coin and he took it.

Though I did a winter's worth,
holding is just not a speed.

And I can walk hard enough to turn.

And no one asks my geopolitics.

And not everything in the water ate me.

I carried the wet, shaking animal in the corner, my heart.

I could hear it.

I'd rather be lucky.

In orchid shades, at your bouquet ready,

at the door—
still and blown out.

A man didn't invent me,

I come with all this.

It's burnt into the structure.
It's banged out at the piano.

It dug into the back of the air.

Let's say, now, outside,
in the field,

I am the vanilla mint you love,

the letting someone
move me, or melting out of it.

The Inventor Takes an X-ray

I am writing
as your wife.

Everything was beginning.

We'd left the cadenza's warmth, left the concert hall.

Christmas scripting the place
and the x of unknown.

They hit us with the certificate,

the first Nobel Prize in Physics.

My job was to hold still,
 it involved the keeping of time,

an actress against the world's best scientific procedure.

—The most certain now questionable.

—A near relative of light.

Though it's not human to,
I loved it.

My chilled limbs fraught with perfect work.

Fresh as a column, like an animal swimming around coral.

I left my body for sleep I could name.

My hands more yours than mine.
That part of me lasts an ancient fossil,

sweet layered, once animal near rocks.

—I am the wife's hand and this wedding ring.
It scares us.

10 is the radius of the inventor. (Unit unknown.)

This is
what we've practiced.

Time I was closest to the surface.

Time I came out so close,

I was right up to the edge and could almost,
from where I was,
reach through.

APRIL IN PARIS

What have you done: wood, unheavy hate,
to my heart: ratty home.
This is the feeling: elite, finest highs.
Never met it face to face: tentative coffee cream.
Heart could sing: ungodliest arch.
My heart could sing: ghastly indecorum.
Whom can I run to: unharmonic two.
Face to face: café to café.
A warm embrace: raw, macabre me,
clawing at the surface of this year.

Metalepsis

There's joy in being set apart, | I heard, there are crystal caves below,
invisible, corner-like— | I knew only the sheen of the page,
in a darkness. How can I change | the pen's making, my fingerprints!
my language to explain— | You sweat in there like you would
had we an easy correspondence | in a vat. It was on a show.
I'd tell you, I am radically gone. | I'd been watching commercials—
Tried to hail a cab. Couldn't see myself | convinced the opposite of ghost was man
getting one. If I were with you, | was your author, was my best light, was
true, you'd speak but wouldn't | this furious dancing, this hobbling man
step past me. When you see yourself | signing autographs before dying offstage
in a mirror, you see limits | —there's no non-ghost, just off-ghost,
I see only an expanse. | ¾ time ghost, perfumed with ghost—
You are boundaries enacted. | Where did I end?

Echo Lake

Rachel used to work here,
so I got the palomino
all afternoon and it got dark.
She plays the accordion, Rachel got to say,
pointing to me,
once we reached the others.
We ran breathless.
We weren't riding anymore.
Growing up on a farm, I expected it to come back.
And years of piano lessons to play this corrido
for the cowboys lighting up marshmallows.
If you told me to take this stick off the ground
and lick it, why I'd do it!
Rachel says. I am like the silent film star in her video
of the campfire and my laugh, like Clara Bow in *Parisian Love*
where she doesn't know how to be a lady
but she wants to.

Carnegie Hall

Lauren Bacall loved it here,
the stage is still dressed with her.

Outside, beside a row of tulips,
yellow as my grandmother's ideas,

two women hold up their signs—
I NEED A TICKET!

One sings to herself,
and the other eyes her.

I don't remember performing
Chopin in a lady's Princeton home—

my piano instructor—she'd saddened into herself,
into the room arranged, a portrait with curtains,

a second applause. I never told her the truth.
I played devil sticks and didn't practice shit.

I think of her like turning cement around.
It's heavy work. The wet ivy of the past.

It's spring
and the flowers' wet heads

are lopped off for market.
White petaled, milk peach,

dolloped, on the nose,
not late, not lowercase.

I wear them
on me,

from yore, made mine,
glass stoppered.

Awfully

Walk through the park like three Andrews Sisters
who put down their milkshakes to walk over in sync.
Tonight, imagine entering door after door, seamlessly
and as without speech as you can. You and he will never
be as alone as you want. The scene is set from a young age
—silk-lined, shined silver, the promised piece of art customs
couldn't decide whether or not to tax. Walk over like a Ptolemy—
in diadem, in gold, in what is beyond you, in power, like a Ptolemy—
There's finality to this, as at the end of an Andrews Sisters song,
the sound of a drum
like a piano shutting
quickly that I love.

Quiet on Set

he is underwater
walking with you

he touches you and in each one you fall out of yourself

woman from the mountain
woman in borrowed shoes

and the shaky name of someone else

like the round, marble scent of rose

you're writing on his shoulder

you finally
resemble
all the chandeliers

II.

Beethoven
Symphony No. 7 in A Major Op 92. Allegretto.

I.

I've come to where you've led me, knee deep in the untouched,
my shoes worn bare.

The night before
was a thin chain around my neck that a man tore off and replaced.

The night before a dress rehearsal of the opera, alone,

before which a man stopped in the street
to touch the hem of my gown.

As if an old soldier I can't fight anymore.
As if mayor
my words take on an edge of decree—

There are 7,000 structurally deficient bridges in America.
The corset too asks questions
of pressure and displacement.

II.

I tell you this in the present of perpetual truth.

Rome's power was not measured
in appropriated lands and cultures,
replenished troops, impressive displays
of war elephants and chariots. It was this—

when Rome told you to do something you'd do it.

We left our bathing suits on the dock. The lakebottom felt like a dessert underfoot.

Grab my hand from underneath.
Behave very honorably
as if you could never forget what you owe. As if
this is the face of experience.

I'd bullied the evening into happening.

I fought with the blade between my teeth to keep happening.

III.

Clement as a
cut grapefruit.

I am a pert soubrette, the minuend.
The human shape—the cursive L.

When I wake up,

it's as if I'd gotten too close
to something
I couldn't see was happening,
as if sunburnt.

IV.

There was to be music, desire of steam.

The band of pennants tied between two trees.
The only way I've known myself all winter,
a piped in piano trio,
escaping through the bowl of the mountain, floor of the forest.

This winter, I've known myself high gothic, Old February,
crowned with a black reach, thick with delicacy, in love
with every trim of grief.

The message on the tombstone read, *much later it makes sense, how's usa?
how's this?*

Fuzz from the carpet, from everybody dancing.

Kierkegaard said terror would help,
perhaps a fear of beauty.

There's something hidden, go and find it.

There's a buzz, a song or the beginning,
the planks of wood, the dust like myrrh,
like some bearing blown up.

There's me, there's a secret, and there's the feeling I am giving it away.

V.

Each day I am a child king, a fat royal, a real set of taste and pirouettes.

This won't help you.

A field of fortune will.

My sister asks if that sadness is mine and if she can sit there anyway.
My sister's body, awfully like mine in its stripes and discomfort and its hope for
        U.S. mail.

VI.

Each day we draw the boat and make it happen.

Each day proves I was spectacularly wrong

as we cross the water in Giotto blue gowns.

Unknowns travel past us, familiar in their perverse origin, their antique ledger notes.

> A man will tear off
> a silver string of hexagons
> from the folklore tree branch
> to show where we've all been.

VII.

The deer has walked this path as me.
The hearts and broken hearts
are evidence she was here.

Snow world I share with deer hooves,
these high heel marks will tell you.

On the hike, I found a buck's antler. It was in my fist
for hours, it scraped my leg, my grip changed.

Wouldn't you like someone? You're like me you've received the terrifying news.

Ripe and fit
for the madhouse.

Branches snap
tethered to ice.

Bands of light dig through.
I become my body exactly.

VIII.

Pines as high as a century.
Fog like stumbling into a van Gogh 'gainst a lime wall.

We opened time
with our hands
the way you know, if you have ever lived

with a grandfather clock, you can.

I gave myself
what I wanted to be true.

I exist only by torch. I stop when I shut it off.

Each night the success of this throat.
I cut bangs. I wore coral.

Each night I am imagined.
I come apart turned down.

The humming before something happens—I was listening,
or there is a word for it, at any rate.

That word loose in my mind as a door handle.

IX.

An aged door is opened by the composer.

Slowly at the forte.

Shocking in a full black skirt, two suede heels,
and a set of stag antlers two feet high.

I know how to walk in them.

If you look up, you get the feel of a hay loft.

We held our frontiers.
Emitted light by the stone fireplace.

If you're lucky you will end up with just a dueling scar,

forget completely what pain is.

Sensitive system, unset structure,
unsteady change.

I am reverent.
Believe in me.

III.

Trieste-Zurich-Paris

Every renegado sad and civil in a suit.

The cities are shoes worn
writing while walking,

and these italics silverblue—
you fill notebooks with their vowel breath.

Open an umbrella,

it's Valentine week.
Those in trenchcoats form a baroque
brick wall.

They unravel a feeling
close to whaling.

Take your hat when you go.
Take your cigarettes hard to the heel
of your hand.

Touching someone else's
spins your umbrella perfect,

this weather like falling into turquoise.

When you finish your great novel
each city italicized will have the feel of seafoam,

the final lapping, as if the ocean were done,
you've hit the shore.

Consider
this subscription permanent, if you like it here.

As Ivy Smith

> "Well, like it says, they pick a new Miss Turnstiles every month.
> Excuse me"
> *–On the Town* (1949)

All of me, all of me, s'marvelous, worth one day.
All the scales, the practiced evenings,
all the modern men who pity
my head in their hands. (Line 1, Literally, "...in inloveness")
All my cells shake themselves
crazy—awake! Rev alone in tire spinning diction. Less
hard and less against you. Less adrenal, less mirthless.
Come see—Ivy and her ludicrous burlesque! All skirt belled,
I too am a world—all steps ruled by a tight stitched hem.
My heels portend the height from which I'll fall. No!
All antlers ram enemies—all strength from my true
and female head. (Line 10, Literally, "...even if lips blend...")
Mise en abyme, tarnished glass. Gene,
my big American, every one is gone.

My Head Magritte Gone

there's no ending just marbles
loosed from the sky like weather

only my hat remains
my face clouds or apples

you want me to stop
drinking like this to just

throw my sombrero in the air with you
everyone's pistol going off the pianist trying not to get shot

I'm the only man here
who's spent any montane time alone

and Colorado had only its seizing
panic had only a return flight home

I scream in bed
so good to be in one piece.

The African Queen (1951)

I didn't have a lamp I didn't think
would burn the place down then.

I held back, no, was held, but very fast
as in a carriage riding all over Russia.

I could reach you as if you
were here. I could build my body

up buddleia, get the best wings
over me. Toss my hat off the boat

when you laugh like that,
like a bonfire in a cave.

That you loved my Intimissimi
with a look of the jeweler's window

lit by electricity, long as an Alfons Mucha,
draped as a lithographed woman,

both directions, sheath of reasons,
proud, perfect, pin-up, architectural

as Christopher Smart's cat—fine
admit what electrical skin meant in 1759.

The Seven Year Itch (1955)

the color bananas and cream
and the Hesperides perfume

my hair blonder in your hands

enter with a paper bag as if of tumbling oranges
hips and wings in stereophonic sound, warning—soft and hygienic,
pure eyelid

attach to an existing person, a real man
brass buttons on his briefcase, the coal scent of leather

or that nervous scent of a cotton candy's vat in the air, someone to meet at
the carnival—
as in
      childhood

really
the whole costume was lipstick, believe me I bled nowhere
anyone could see not even me

but it's more a feeling, look!
—I am here, a real prayer

clean of existing, loose of that god's eye
if he saw me tonight I'd be a basket of fresh white pleated hellos!

The Nude as Champagne Swallow

Sure it's a crime.
Features rare as a fir tree's.
The round high ass, the modern applied arts,
the blank side of a correspondence card.
My hot longshoreman,
sure,   here she is.

A gewgaw to you, not substantial enough
to crush garlic under a knife, a showy flower.
Hand holding a shallow champagne glass,
a tiny smoking woman.

Your eyes are the color of information,
and if this grief had more energy to it I wouldn't
be seated, semi-nude, facing left, female
with mirror in right hand.

You found me
bucket eyed, a stuffed animal,
the silver chalice of leftover milkshake,
your hat check girl, the fat Wagner of my
German face, a fog you ate, the best thing
you did for your lungs.

As Vera-Ellen

> "She must be pretty important!"
> "Oh, I wouldn't say that."
> —*On the Town* (1949)

This is what will be what was
—cut my silhouette

into this other door of living.

Stage lights, then nothing.

My tongue in the bare cup of my mouth

like a dancer with a marble hall to fill.

I stand astonished   as if someone in the audience has
suggested my line.

We'd done all this training
in January's Chinatown,
frost scraping my limbs.

To survive
we keep on one light.

Let this be more
than the courtly love   of the anacreontic anorectic,

I love to be winked at in kindness.

Love your acute, foolhardy moves around my dress—

You're a nut to ignore everyone else.

I can hold my drink like royal tusk jewelry
and an entire man in my arms.

I feel I've hurt you somehow: emotive, hourly housewife.

wait—

Say I wrote you.

Exotica

In his early films, someone's always
hungry, someone drives in silence,
the handsome hero puts his hands
on his wife's head so she'll stop spinning.
The surprise machine eats her quarter,
an egg becomes. As the Met is fooled
the acquisition is real. As she won't
look directly into the photograph of the sun.
Belief becomes her. She builds a speech
of darting across the red street. He sits
down as if coming from an awful hunting
accident. As Teddy Roosevelt's
horns, mounted tusks, leopard coats
become things one shouldn't covet.

With Seamed Stockings

The dead trees stand just like the living, like
an ivy covered pergola of lanterns. Come here.

I will otherwise return, grab my head, stare at
my computer like Gustave Courbet's Self-Portrait.

You'd think there'd be a scent beyond the watch,
swath of metal on skin and the heat of its compounds,

when you reach an age. If I fell asleep,
would it take a century to melt?

I am the age of an old horse.
My handwriting is not unlike

Edith Wharton's. You are about
70 degrees with distinct fall light.

You are like that German word that
means the world feels like it's collapsing.

It (1927)

    I. [Starring Clara Bow]

A bunch of peaches stand behind the counter,

in their heat identified hair, finger waves.

Mink lashes, foxfur, dropwaist, a curl to the cheek.

All the shopgirls at work,
and the new boss!

Clara drops her spool and we can see she's in love,
      in her cloche and concave chest.

Her eyes grow large enough to fit me inside.

She gets a few extra
seconds alone, then makes short work of the new boss.

II. [Boss takes It Girl out on the town, or *Old fruit—you've got IT!*]

–Come to Coney Island with me–

The fun house with the floor that spins us abeam.

Come into the rowboat that manifests you against me,

     and a slide where I'll hold you in your corset.

I can see your bloomers in the turning barrel.

Silent movie cry, jaunty miss.
     Wasn't that perfect and happy and strange?

It won't end badly, will it? Who will buy you yachting clothes?

III. [Windy Yacht Scene, Clara meets her beau's fiancée but remains positive]

I'm all arms out funny and skinny, the way you want?

She's a ripping sort, really, positively top-heavy with 'IT'

So smeared around the edge and down, a long line,

rather lacking in reserve—that's what

I was always good at. Always good at being a hard bite,
    at being mid-ocean perfect.

It means so much to me right now—if we are alive.

I've something to say, take the wheel, Monty!

Off the boat, the women hold on to one another
    —or are they trying to drown each other?

I had to knock her cold, she says, of the other, Adela,
    ornate with need and redundancy

in her wet skirts, graphic, and not enough for the audience,
    clapping to the original piano score.

The It Girl ends on the prow of the *Itola*,
    hanging off an anchor, freezing with want
    of nothing.

With Boots

I'm like the horse
when you give him an apple.

Like Hafiz chanting *now now now*
      when he wants   what?

This is it.
Know if we change the music we'll stop.

The voice, you can't not hear it,
           a bass footprint to step in.

More inside and inside the original orchestration.
More inside the grand hall.

Sit down and take off that weary shirt.

Assume the aspect of the philosopher.

I've added rings of living to my torso.
Cut me in half to prove it.

If a real cowboy,
a real cowboy would.

On the Town (1949)

Knowing is unbearable
                    when I get it right.

One to another to another to find you.

When I did
I kissed the door

that you closed near
the side of my face.

We made a fuss over you and your small honor,
Miss Turnstiles—

I kept saying I disappear.
                    I disappear when this ends, but

there's something that doesn't
and it's that I never disappeared. Really, to myself.

We ran out
and afterward that night wasn't running out.

We were close to the dancing girls who
closed the place down and you leaned in,

                    one arm over me, reaching.

Roped to happiness.

A sailor picked a girl for one day.
A woman who could stand on her head, every strength.
The most famous in New York City, listed for one month.

Each fact made you witness to me.
Fin.

The actress
in a turban like a foxglove—
we'd like a skyline
through our chests,
one made of her,
sympathetic, parasympathetic, sin,
synapse—angel food,
closer to nature.
How? World class reason will not answer
this question—
ask limited questions so we can be happy,
ask me—
I'll answer by
my downturned mouth.
She is a skyline design—
He almost walks back
to his guests naked—
There is no Garbo!
There is no Dietrich!
There is

Kekulé dreamed of
a serpent of perspicacity—
an ouroboros
an arrangement of atoms;
Samuel Johnson dreamed and risked
defining all in a director's chair—
he tumesced with epiphenomena—
Kant on a cliff, super, set in motion—
afraid—ballyhoo, worldly-minded;
we doff our hat, cigar, tie to
have a cupreous reputation;
eye to the keyhole;
the sound of fire—a matte vision—
Monosyllabic, reduced. Lo.
Nutcracker snow falls;
when she turns the camera
on herself—
she isn't there;
she's run offstage.
One consonant left to her name.

Double Indemnity (1944)

Having a husband   is a problem at this time.

And a woman's a problem because she'll want you to keep seeing her.

I think I like that
        —but you're not sure.

Like last night's cigars and daylight, perhaps it was worth it to me.

We turned on the wrong street and gave the signal.

Living now
                        exists under another name.

Honeysuckle also called hysteria.

A flame in soft focus.

I woke the next day,
                kept looking over my shoulder.

Slouchy and keen, you enjoy your surroundings like a wolverine.

                Another part ready to be played and as fancy a piece—

                I ran smack into the woman I am now.

How to Marry a Millionaire (1953)

In a series of beveled mirrors,
what comes from an object
belongs to the surface, as

from my grandmother
to me, to a hundred
years. The image

severs the contract between us.
Part my hair the wrong way,
I'm no longer her.

A cheap song runs through
me and a fear of spectacles.
I can't see and can't be seen

in them, is the gag. Wisdom,
an unwelcome irritant.
Hot rollers,

so near my ears,
a fireplace's poker.
The room can wait.

I never wanted
to be unliked:
weakened, nutritive blonde.

Schatze says, "I'm getting nostalgic
—you smell like Pola right now,"
like I was already gone.

Last night, a female cab driver stopped
for me. Each car passed and honked
through the light as she waited.

A Fool There Was (1915)

The movie opens with a slight tear—

Theda Bara had already told the lie of hookah in her hair,
she'd stylized her thin black mouth and the white hands.

Runa Hodges, her sausage curls lash wickedly behind her ears,
a kitten to everyone's arms.

In this movie, every female becomes chipped china with grief
and he loses it all, you knew that much.

Runa Hodges says, I'm scared to be a grown up in the dark.

The nurse is here, as is the silver pitcher.
        She brings the newspaper, a throwaway.

He sails tomorrow.

Bonton, tintype, ribbon head, striking head.

We'd drop dead if you were to tell us it all at once.

It seems, Runa, you don't have to be you yet
        when everyone picks you up
        and tosses you around.

A stagy rose, a slim pistol.

In a film like this, the men ruin all the furniture in the room.

They can't stop until every glass is broken and their hands are bleeding
and the friends are watching and their fortune outlives them and the
anger is a waste and the boat is waiting.

The moon emerges from the porthole, like the Moon After Yule.

An ostrich feather in the wind, everything secured by hatpins.
Everyone wave.

As Miss Turnstiles

Toylike
through
the veil of highball.

Struck
though
I still walked around.

Part heat,
part grief,

a streak,
something
not human
in me.

Drunk on
sailors and
a fame that ends.

A surprise:
as is purer.

The limited body of ancient data.
The finite body of a short woman.

I had to
mother
myself out of the house.

Absinthe Makes the Heart Grow Fonder

They were playing my song when we stepped into the bar
—I grabbed Monika's wrist, come to papa, come to papa.

That song had just been in the sunlit corner of my bedroom.

It started playing back when you would hit record,
the moment too good to not make yours.

Back in radio, back in the hardwood house,
when you called into the station to answer

"Reading Gaol" to win tickets.
The applause and a cough came through, like someone was
actually in the room.

As if in the bar with us,
a musician takes a breath in the recording.

My green heart records
Eudaimonia—or an understanding of that word.

I too would haunt this room.

Δ*Time*

Now,
        the unfamiliar cast of mind
becomes pine,
        moonshine, and the high alcohol
        of my blood.
Who would be there—
        anticipation
of the opera, seeing
        and being seen,
        is a feeling extinct
except in some sectors,
        like, here—
a barefoot youth,
        unknown,
        steps into what would be my kitchen.
She manages hot toddies on a stove
        I once leaned against
and drunk said
        who knows what,
        not yet climatized to critique,
not yet the smaller, sooner reward.
        I desired to desire to hold
myself upright, to shout through
        Mayakovsky's megaphone
        of my youth.
I'd learn to behave
        and change my head.
We met as tourists.
        Each edge was not a joke,
        like they are now.
My psychosocial swain.
        My bawdy love with your pearl
handled pistol patrolling the hall.
        You left for town
        and left and
never came back.
        It isn't the lack, (remind us)

not the ship or the rival ship,
          the possible
expanding, but all apodicticity
          that can't be heard. So what
never had to
end can end.

Against Remorse

In Germany for the film premiere,
I missed my transfer and ended up in Bissendorf,

where I ate an apple and read from a book on which I'd spilled a tall
    glass of water.
The paper had become ancient, authoritative, thin—

the voice spoke from a wavy place
in honeysuckle air.

I thought when you smelled something that good,
something that good was coming to you, that old belief.

It was unbolted late summer and I was falsifiable, pure id.
I carried Louise Brooks with me everywhere,

kept paying for her way in,
had her spin hot on my lap.

I made us pose under her framed portrait, once I met the others.
We entered the old theater I'd imagined.

The movie starred my fullscreen face, my every fear.
In épaulement, large against the sky like a philosopher who looked
    upset,
like she could tear a book in two.

After the film, we spoke.
My voice came back idealized

with a topaz sound. A feeling of being in English. Parts fell away.

How to connect to this elaborate address, borrowed?
World, I'm trying to believe. I said.

I held the mic like a bouquet.

Monk's Dream

               The divine skull,
the thick skull, the skull of registry glass,
I mean regency crystal, of which I know little,
the thing with which I used to play that was my
grandmother's, that was her ashtray, that wasn't a thing
with which for me to play but for her ring, the skull a major
triad, the skull legato, the thin seminary drapes, the skull alone
in the cathedral, skull of my gold pen in its looped name, ascending
a flight of stairs. Hear someone's improv piano. It gets louder each floor
but it's loudest right above you. Just through the ceiling one floor up. Keeping
you. You'd like to find the musician making home of some top stair. The staircase
has a warm, still smell of a children's library. Whenever you can, come, no matter
what day.

Like Sheet Music

I.

A woman loses her mind all over the piano
and shouts when she plays.

There is nothing else I am supposed to be doing right now.

A stern woman turns the sheet music
as a name is said into the lit air of the concert hall.

I kept thinking as a kid I could do it, didn't I feel that way?

I am colder now, proper,
full of flop-eared devotion.

A long stillness on my face.
Long on the simmered breathing, carbonated blood.

Don't you know what it is to be a salesman?
The composer nods yes,
nods no to the violinist.

II.

I must sit in your room like sheet music.

Pizzicato panic then

a crisp cut of silence unfolds you back away from me.

I stopped in a secondhand store to remember a name,

as the hornman and the organ have only been here sad,

as we hear a bar of Art Tatum's EMBRACEABLE YOU from around
the corner,

as the night is a candle put out by rain.

Like Lotte wiping dust off of the pistol, just hand it here,
      we'll put it away.

I remember as a kid crossing wires—someone else on the phone.

III.

I forget how it sounds when I don't say your name.

Shackled by my sight of you. Motion blind.

Your call, your letter:
or true cruel loyalty.

I promised a cannon of myself.

How powerful that guarantee,
it really goes.

The age in which we live reminds you.

All Your Fears Are Foolish

Maybe if I come with you.
If I trudge up to my knees, leave what's abandoned behind.

Work is a kind of love: now, of silkier vodka,
no longer an orphan with one sock.

If it can smell like fireplace everywhere
tonight.

I'll bring a luxe sable the length of me. I'll bring apples in my skirt.

If it makes sense to Pa.
If it arrives with a laugh.

If I keep running,
the entire field house to myself, my heart like a vole stuck in a shoebox.

If it is, ribs of firewood will cower.
I'll sing MY MELANCHOLY BABY wrong.

You can read it coming off of me.

Two Stanza Republic

A baby calls out from each room.
Chubby cheeks, it's in the bag,
I know ten bright-eyed ways to start a breakfast.
Borrowed and blue,
pregnant as a 19th century hot air balloon,
no longer just a pretty face,
right here. This longing

ahum. For this house,
we used all the wood
from the broken deer blind
the drunken farmer had knocked down.
I identified with something for so long
I thought was me, but was youth instead.
I like this farm
life it's not permanent.

To Have and Have Not (1944)

He addresses this body

the way a firefighter
addresses an elevator
he must operate
within a burning building.

You know, I was not born in
a cabbage patch.

It's that time we part.

I have to join the gang at the piano.
It's urgent. They need me to sing right away.
Listen,

I don't care how much room I take up.

LHOOQ.
Give me a bateria.

This exclamation point means everything
I've just said multiplied by itself, getting smaller!

IT'S ONLY A PAPER MOON

THERE's   no   pit   beneath   you.
Some   air current unknown until then
supports.   You   are   an   amazing   sight   reader
with no rehearsal time   expected to perform.
It's what was always happening.

Someone came to you   like he had his mind
on something else.   Like you were a kitten
                          in a yellow barrette.

Trouble of this sort is not an alternate take.   You don't say
Oh you don't say! You let him in   you were too
gentle, to a fault, to a cat.   You don't say you
shouldn't have treated him like   he wasn't going to eat
you alive.

Everything you thought   before
                          shouts   then   runs

away.

That present tense deceives.   You therefore
cannot ever again be   considered a minor
actress.

A FEMININE ENDING

ITALICIZED anything says, *I've kept enough secret.* It exploits a basic fact. By *all of us,* Freud means men; *all of us* connotes only those intensely interested in the neural basis of thought and behavior. Barrier is feminine. We can assume weapons are feminine like countries, like kiss prints. Le rêve is masculine. It lurches late in the scene wearing a tight suit. They warned you, right?

Historic hurricanes. Ships. Hitchcock asked around for one. A hand, please. Demure is a word, as is coy, as is eager. Radio, me. I arrive by the dinner bell of a diamond ring. I followed the decree of the local satrap. I have an ice cream cone and a "men's" shirt and all my hair in a hat. Just as the tulip petal grew into the neural tube, anagram for your poet, this brain grew to expect something missing.

The Film is Now Considered Lost

ANACHRONISMS—
I held up electric hands.

Letter delayed, you called.

CHARACTER ERROR—
To wound others, they said,
　　　use your first look.

I look cross in that scene.

EQUIPMENT VISIBLE—
The cilia and baby-fat of Ophelia.

They dropped an iris and tulip bouquet
　　　on my head.

ERRORS IN GEOGRAPHY—
The director rubbed his hands in the grass's
　　　rain to keep my hair like that.

REVEALING MISTAKES—
The director stood on a chair

and dropped my book on my head

—they couldn't use the footage.

STORYLINE—
I never looked when I knew where it was,

the movie that opened with my face.

CONTINUITY—
Always in that movie

you run right into me.

Doubtful Attribution

To bear meaning is a perk of being

a noblewoman in the Middle Ages.

That's not it. As hero worshipper

is to the delicate human onstage,

as outside your body isn't a bad

place to be. A mind of phrases

is to Voltaire's fifteen million

word corpus and not through

touch, as to understand is to

relate more to me before I

could speak, which is a

quality that "kills men"

my boss tells me. Not it.

How to be less demimondaine.

THE MAN I LOVE

This day we're living in,
this part where the man I love in his hat, in front of trees,
in front of the theater, lit up with stringed bulbs,
appears a negative, what isn't there is him, the man I love.
The man I love,
shy in the corner, tuning something.
Oh, I can't afford it, will it never come back?
They cannot be removed, right?
Fervid with sophistry, dreamy for you,
but not for me.
Any Russian play, a fool to fall and get that way.
Starstruck at the roar of his railroad,
the man I love.
Follow my lead.
Maybe, let's say,
I could always be good.
One strawberry left. That's yours.
We both won't say a word.
We braid what we know
with what we don't, like a crossword.
I've caught you playing the museum's piano.
It is in splendid playing condition,
with light, responsive action.
Rosewood Satinwood Purpleheart.
We've spent our lives
seated on delicate side chairs, and
can barely see the pianist.
He takes everyone home from here.

La Mujer del Puerto (1934)

A silken cord drops a curtain
to reveal the only girl in town.

The movie blinks for you.

A hearty stranger
I've never known is here.

I dug deep to live like this, and now this boat
ferries me from what I can touch to what I can't.

Meanwhile,
he dries his boots
under the antique piano.

Meanwhile, beloved
finds himself against what never could, against
me.

He carries the news in his mouth,
sets fire to it three times.

He says,

My dearest Girl,
        Relieve me
        the weight
        of my head.

Rain like a spray over the bow,
my best shoes for a downpour.

The study of damage
accentuated by water.
Like poppy to me,
I fall into it.

As the Dark Ages

Handed from barbarian to barbarian.

The Burgundian Code says
if they pull my hair with only one hand
they're free.

I carry what I own over
my ovibovine shoulders.

In my stone home, doing a book, copying
the work, keeping things, illustrating
the corners with spilled water,

hiding under the table.

Mix of miracle and sap.

I eat the grains
out of my sack with my tongue and hands, many blocks home.

When they want something, the monarchs raise their arms.
The edge shivers.

I want something,
namely,
to be out of The Dark Ages.

Its name like a joke that fills you with awe.

Stepping Out

The CO_2 plume rises from your obvious
attendance. 5 a.m. by yourself.

I approach you in the field
and you stare back in what I take as terror.

You give away,
and think before you give away
only in your dreams.

You thought you could come out
but it was too early.

Seafoam spun from my own brain.
Body, you knew the surprise
was to happen.

Upright as champagne in the snow,
a dancer's feel top and down.

If someone tried to push you over you'd
hardly move.

I take credit for your beauty,
as if I grew it myself.

ACKNOWLEDGMENTS

My gratitude to the editors of the following publications in which poems first appeared sometimes in a slightly different form:

Alaska Quarterly Review, "To Have and Have Not"
Anti-, "With Seamed Stockings"
Berkeley Poetry Review, "As Tolstoy's Natasha on the Hunt"
Black Warrior Review, "The Announcement"
Boxcar Poetry Review, "Echo Lake"
Civil Coping Mechanisms Compendium 2015-16, "Problem of Plague"
The Cortland Review, "Exotica"
The Doctor T. J. Eckleburg Review, "My Head Magritte Gone"
Entropy, Selections from "Beethoven," "Like Sheet Music"
Gulf Coast, "Two Stanza Republic"
Harvard Review Online's Poetry Pick; "The Platonic What's at Stake"
Hunger Mountain, "Hard Hat," "Wanted as Handled"
Jeffery Berg's National Poetry Month Feature, 2014, "Awfully"
The Journal, "It Sails Off"
Literary Orphans, "Monk's Dream"
Lumina, "Birthday," "The African Queen," "Trieste-Zurich-Paris"
Massachusetts Review, "As the Dark Ages"
Minola Review, "Claude Thornhill Arrangement"
The Nervous Breakdown, "Spare a Traveler Some?"
New Ohio Review, "It"
North American Review, "Binary"
The Pinch, "As Fats Waller as Me"
Prelude Online, "As Vera-Ellen," "Red Paisley," "The Seven Year Itch"
Prelude (Print), "Double Indemnity," "On the Town," "ΔTime"
Redivider; "The Nude as Champagne Swallow"
Sonora Review, "Metalepsis"
The Westchester Review, "As Aubrey Beardsley"
3:AM Magazine, "As Ivy Smith," "As Miss Turnstiles"

Eternally grateful to the following—Rebecca Azenberg, for chamber music, symphonic music, all in between. Hannah Beresford, for poet-heart wisdom. Chase Berggrun, for your willingness to always read a seconds-old draft. Kay Cosgrove, the most elegant in Grand Central, for so much of this was written next to you. Nick Criscuolo, for anagrams. Stephen Danay, thank you for sending me The Petrified Forest through the post to the forest. Adrianna de Svastich, for your magic. Carina del Valle Schorske, for your Grown Woman prompts. Dionissios Kollias, for seeking art with me, listening to the pianist play La Vie en Rose. T Kira Ching Madden, for your typewritten letters, your loyalty, best model of friendship. Varun Mehra for being family. Rachel Morgese, for horses and the dream of the farm.

Keen readers of a thousand drafts, Monika Anderson, Michael Christian, Lucy Hitz, thank you for your sweetness and laughter and insight. You all made this book real.

Thank you to the amazing team at the SPRUNGBRETT Workshop and the up-and-coming International Film Festival in Hannover, Germany. Thank you to all my friends, teachers, the folks at Young Writers Workshop, heroes of No Tokens, MacDowell pals, I love you.

Thank you, Larry Krone, for this perfect cover, perfect parties, and your aesthetic appreciation of opening credits. Dean Bartoli Smith, for your belief in this project. Deep respect to Michael J. Seidlinger for your tireless and prevailing faith in books.

My whole heart to the MacDowell Colony and the Virginia Center for the Creative Arts, where I began these poems and completed them. Thank you for your generosity, kindness, and support. Without the hardworking people keeping those places heaven, none of this would be possible.

To my family. I love you! This book is for you.

OFFICIAL

CCM ◗

GET OUT OF JAIL
* VOUCHER *

- -

Tear this out.

Skip that social event.

It's okay.

You don't have to go if you don't want to. Pick up
the book you just bought. Open to the first page.

You'll thank us by the third paragraph.

If friends ask why you were a no-show, show them
this voucher.

You'll be fine.

- -

We're coping.

◗

CPSIA information can be obtained at www.ICGtesting.com
Printed in the USA
BVOW08s2146191016

465529BV00001B/43/P

9 781937 865764